The Church
Recovery Guide

The Church Recovery Guide

How Your Congregation Can Adapt and Thrive after a Crisis

Karl Vaters

MOODY PUBLISHERS
CHICAGO

Some content was adapted from articles featured on KarlVaters.com, NewSmallChurch.com, and *Pivot*, a blog by Karl Vaters (https://www.christianitytoday.com/karl-vaters/).

All Scripture quotations, unless otherwise indicated, are taken from the Holy Bible, New International Version®, NIV®. Copyright © 1973, 1978, 1984, 2011 by Biblica, Inc.™ Used by permission of Zondervan. All rights reserved worldwide. www.zondervan .com. The "NIV" and "New International Version" are trademarks registered in the United States Patent and Trademark Office by Biblica, Inc.™

Scripture quotations marked NASB are taken from the New American Standard Bible® (NASB), Copyright © 1960, 1962, 1963, 1968, 1971, 1972, 1973, 1975, 1977, 1995 by The Lockman Foundation. Used by permission. www.Lockman.org.

Scripture quotations marked (NLT) are taken from the Holy Bible, New Living Translation, copyright ©1996, 2004, 2015 by Tyndale House Foundation. Used by permission of Tyndale House Publishers, a Division of Tyndale House Ministries, Carol Stream, Illinois 60188. All rights reserved.

Scripture quotations marked KJV are taken from the King James Version.

Edited by Mackenzie Conway
Interior and cover design: Erik M. Peterson
Cover image of flashlight copyright © 2019 by Boris Rabtsevich / Shutterstock (1166022700). All rights reserved.

Library of Congress Control Number: 2020939514

ISBN: 978-0-8024-2343-6

Originally delivered by fleets of horse-drawn wagons, the affordable paperbacks from D. L. Moody's publishing house resourced the church and served everyday people. Now, after more than 125 years of publishing and ministry, Moody Publishers' mission remains the same—even if our delivery systems have changed a bit. For more information on other books (and resources) created from a biblical perspective, go to: www .moodypublishers.com or write to:

Moody Publishers
820 N. LaSalle Boulevard
Chicago, IL 60610

1 3 5 7 9 10 8 6 4 2

Printed in the United States of America

CONTENTS

INTRODUCTION

Nothing will ever be the same again.

That's true every single day of our lives. Even in relatively stable times, we awake each morning to a world that is slightly different than it was the day before.

The advantage of the incremental changes we usually face is that we have the chance to adapt to them with only minor disruptions. The disadvantage is that the disruptions are often so minor as to be unnoticeable, so we don't make the necessary adaptations until it's too late.

With the massive disruptions we're facing as a result of the COVID-19 crisis of 2020 and beyond, the problems could not be more disruptive or obvious. From the lockdowns, to the unspeakable pain of the illness and death of loved ones, to the colossal financial upheavals, it is likely that we've never faced such a long-term disruption in our lifetimes, possibly even surpassing those that resulted from the terrorist attacks of September 11, 2001.

The size and scope of these current disruptions also mean that we can't ignore the need for immediate and permanent changes any longer. We must act and adapt. We can't do business, or church, as usual any more.

While the foundational truths of the Bible are as important and reliable as they've always been, the means by which we communicate them are changing more quickly and obviously than ever. Churches that swore they'd never go online, are. Programs we thought we needed, we don't. Congregations that thought they were strong and healthy, aren't.

Meanwhile, some churches, ministries, and individual Christians are not just stepping up to this need, they're thriving as they find new ways to communicate the eternal truths of the gospel through new methods, both digital and analog. But how are they doing this? Let's take a look at why people engage with church in the first place.

TRANSFORMATION AND STABILITY

People go to church for two reasons.

Reason 1: To radically change their life.

Reason 2: To connect with someone who never changes.

Transformation and stability. Two contrasting goals that people expect to get from the same place—no wonder pastoring is so hard.

So who's right? The church as change agent? Or the church as a stable foundation?

Both.

The church needs to be a transformative community. And the church needs to stand for eternal truths. Any church that sacrifices eternal truths for current trends is making a big mistake. And any church that refuses to change their methods to reach a new generation with eternal truths is just as wrong. One is too trendy to last. The other is too outdated to be helpful.

> **WHEN TIMES ARE NORMAL, LEADERS INSPIRE CHANGE.**
>
> **WHEN TIMES ARE DISRUPTIVE, LEADERS PROVIDE STABILITY.**

Most churches emphasize one or the other. We need churches that push us forward in innovative ways, and we need congregations that provide stable, traditional reminders of what we've always been about. But the healthiest churches provide a mix of both. And the wisest pastors and leaders know how to toggle back and forth between the two, emphasizing each when they're needed the most.

When times are normal, leaders inspire change.

When times are disruptive, leaders provide stability.

Right now, times are disruptive. Change is inevitable. The church needs the consistency of strong, steady leaders who can help us negotiate through rough, uncertain waters with biblical truths, passionate hearts, and moral integrity.

Now is not the time for church leaders to cause further disruption, but to help us see a stable path through it. That's where we'll find not just the ability to recover, but the ability to adapt and thrive, no matter what comes next.

CHAPTER 1

IMPACT: WHAT WE KNOW— AND WHAT WE DON'T KNOW

During my forty-plus years of pastoral ministry, I've been asked a lot of questions. Some are easy to answer, others leave me scratching my head.

I used to stress over the hard questions. Or give pat answers. Or take a stab at an answer and hope I was right. I don't do that anymore, since I learned the value of three wonderful words: I. Don't. Know.

I've been using those words a lot lately.

"Are we underreacting, overreacting, or properly reacting to this crisis?"

I don't know.

"When will things get back to normal?"

I don't know.

"What will the church look like going forward?"

I don't know.

WHY "I DON'T KNOW" MATTERS

Strong, decisive leadership matters—especially in a crisis. But more than anything else, people need one characteristic from their leaders when life takes a sideways turn: honesty. There is no more essential element to life, faith, and leadership than the mandate to tell the truth.

An honest "I don't know" is always better than false bravado. After a while, people will see through the false front. And when they do, they will lose trust.

It feels counterintuitive that admitting our ignorance will build trust. We think we'll lose people's trust if we don't have all the answers. The opposite is almost always true. Saying "I don't know" when you don't have an answer lets people know you're not faking it when you do have an answer. People are more willing to trust leaders who are honest about their vulnerabilities than those who only show their strengths.

Plus, especially in times of crisis, fake or simplistic answers can hurt people. When people ask their pastor hard questions, the stakes are often very high. Their health or their faith might be hanging in the balance. This is not the time to spitball it.

If we really know the answer, we should give it. But if we don't, a fake or pat answer can send people down a bad path. It's less dangerous to be ignorant than wrong.

Besides, saying "I don't know" is not the same as saying "God doesn't know." We don't know

THERE IS NO MORE ESSENTIAL ELEMENT TO LIFE, FAITH, AND LEADERSHIP THAN THE MANDATE TO TELL THE TRUTH.

everything God knows. We honor Him when we admit that. Some answers will never be learned this side of heaven. Why COVID-19? I don't know. No one does.

But there are some things we do know. Some things we've always known. The road ahead will be built on the foundation of these eternal truths.

RECALIBRATE CHURCH

The church is not dying. It's in fine shape. Jesus said He'd build it, and He is. Relentlessly and beautifully. But individual congregations, denominations, and ideologies? Now that's another story.

While the church of Jesus around the world continues to move forward, chasing away the darkness with the light of Jesus, many local expressions of the church are watching their candles flicker in recent years. I believe the next decade or two will be critical for the Western church. The culture around us is experiencing a once-in-a-millennium shift right now—a recalibration of the way we think about everything from morality to sexuality, identity, and theology.

So what's the local church to do? We must hold two seemingly competing ideals in our hands at the same time.

Ideal #1: Stand strong on the unchanging principles of God's Word.

Ideal #2: Adapt our methods to a fast-changing world.

If we hope to do these two things well, local congregations must reinforce the following ten principles. And the sooner we get to work on them, the better. The current crisis didn't cause the need to recalibrate the way we do church, but it is accelerating it.

1. Reestablish the biblical essentials

According to an article from the *Washington Post*, churches that stand firm on the biblical essentials are more likely to be thriving, while those that compromise on them are more likely to be dying.[1]

We shouldn't need a newspaper article to tell us to stick to the essentials. While everything else can change, the essentials cannot. Any church that abandons biblical principles won't just fail to survive, it doesn't deserve to.

2. Emphasize discipleship and leadership training

The days of hiring a team of pastors to do all the ministry of the church is dying. Good riddance. Instead, churches that thrive are taking Ephesians 4:11–12 seriously by equipping God's people to do the work of ministry and raising up a team of ministers.

In the coming decades, the pastor's main task must shift from preaching and caregiving, to training lay leaders to do the ministry of the church. That has always been our calling anyway. Events on the ground are now forcing us to do it the biblical way.

For many, maybe most churches, this will be a long-term turnaround of attitudes and methods. Start now, or you may miss the boat.

3. Reduce your overhead

By all accounts, giving trends are down and will continue to fall. This was true even before the COVID-19 lockdowns caused many people to face unexpected cutbacks or layoffs from work. These recent losses are likely to have deep, long-term implications for many years to come. Churches with top-heavy staffing, excessive mortgages, and high-maintenance bills will find themselves buried under their increasing weight in the coming decades.

THE CURRENT CRISIS DIDN'T CAUSE THE NEED TO RECALIBRATE THE WAY WE DO CHURCH, BUT IT IS ACCELERATING IT.

If local congregations, denominations, and parachurch ministries hope to survive, they need to get to work on:

- Getting out of debt (including mortgage)
- Reducing the percentage of budget for paid staff
- Training and empowering volunteers to lead and serve

- Sharing expenses with other churches and ministries
- Preparing ministers-in-training for the likelihood that they will be bivocational

Anything else that can reduce the financial burden of church maintenance is helpful. (We'll look more deeply into these financial issues in chapter 6.)

4. Rethink your building

Until very recently, if someone wanted to start a business, one of the first things they would do was find or build a store, office, warehouse, or other physical structure. Not anymore. Today, the rule is to avoid the encumbrance of a physical building for as long as possible. Churches need to do the same. If your church doesn't have a building, don't be in a hurry to buy one. Stay nimble as long as possible.

If you own a building—especially if you're one of the growing number of churches that own a too-big building for your shrinking congregation—be relentless about finding creative ways to utilize the space as often as possible.

For many of our churches, it's *use-it-or-lose-it* time. As in, use the building or lose the church—facility, people . . . *everything*.

5. Work with strategic partners

In many places, smaller churches are banding together—even across denominational lines—to share resources, think strategically, mend old wounds, and minister to their shared community. In addition, there is a small but growing network of parachurch organizations that are increasingly willing to come alongside local churches for little or no money to share everything from outreach ideas to administrative assistance, to graphic design and more.

Start by asking around on social media. You may be surprised what you'll find. Or start a network yourself. It's easier to do now than it's ever been.

6. Engage your community

Churches must stop being identified by the location of their building. And we can't replace it by being identified for our online presence. We must be recognized for the passion of our heart.

A church that's known as "the people who love kids" (or addicts, or single moms) has a much higher likelihood of thriving and surviving than the church that's known as "the old building on the corner of First and Main" or even "the church with the cool, interactive website."

7. Emphasize Jesus over tradition (or denominations, or buildings, or politics, or . . .)

Everything but Jesus and the Bible must be on the table. Ask yourself this question. "Would I be willing to give up (insert a preference here) if it meant doing a better job of reaching our community for Jesus?" If anything you'd put in that blank makes you pause (other than the biblical essentials), it's an idol that must be abandoned.

For instance, several years ago I was preaching through 1 Timothy. When I came to the mandate to pray for "kings and all those in authority," I offered a prayer that mentioned key people in those positions, including the voters, the mayor, the governor, and so on. I referred to the president and his family by name, asking God to give him wisdom, and to give them a peaceable home life. (No, I won't tell you which president.) I also used the opportunity to encourage the congregation to be careful not to let political beliefs take a higher priority in their lives than our Christian witness.

One church member was so angry about this that he told me he would leave the church if I didn't publicly retract my prayer, condemn the president, and renounce my statement about how to reprioritize our political beliefs. I wouldn't, so he and his family left the church. I'm still saddened when I recall that incident, but our public Christian witness and the scriptural mandate, which includes the phrase "that we may live peaceful and quiet lives in all godliness and holiness" (1 Tim. 2:1–2), was greater than the idol he had made out of his hatred for the president.

8. Restructure what needs to be restructured

Quit fighting to keep your favorite ministry, method, or tradition alive. If it's not part of the solution, it's part of the problem.

9. Make disciples, not just converts

Converts join a club. Disciples start a movement.

Converts follow traditions. Disciples follow Jesus.

Converts change their minds. Disciples change their lives. And other people's lives.

10. Figure out why your congregation should survive

If your church disappeared tomorrow, what would really be lost? Yes, that's a hard question. It might even feel cruel and uncaring. But it's not. It's essential. Any congregation that can't readily answer why they should survive, won't.

START TODAY

It's been said that the best time to plant a tree is twenty years ago—the second best time is today. The same goes for these principles. If you've been doing them, strengthen them. If not, get started now, then be relentless at them. Not just this year, but every year.

The survival of your local church depends on it.

CHAPTER 2

RECONNECTING: COMING BACK FROM QUARANTINE

There are a lot of books and articles that help us understand how a healthy church should behave. That's appropriate. We should always have a picture of our desired future in our hearts and minds.

But what does a pastor do with an unhealthy church? Maybe your church was cruising along before the pandemic, but you knew there were serious problems beneath the surface. When the crisis hit, suddenly those problems became obvious. I'm going to propose a radical idea that shouldn't be considered radical at all: unhealthy churches should be pastored differently than healthy churches. Because unhealthy churches aren't like healthy ones, acting as though they are doesn't help them; it hurts them.

FOUR PROVEN STRATEGIES FOR THE CARE AND TREATMENT OF AN UNHEALTHY CHURCH

Someone with two healthy legs is able to stand, walk, and jump. But treating a broken leg as if it's not broken will hurt it, not help it. If the medical issue is serious enough, the patient is put in an Intensive Care Unit to get closer attention. The same goes for churches. Some churches need to be put in a spiritual ICU.

Unhealthy churches should be treated differently than healthy ones if they have any hope of recovery. But too often we tell hurting, broken, unhealthy churches to start acting like their strong, healthy siblings. Some church leaders approach hurting church members like one of those win-at-all-costs, sports-obsessed parents, with the equivalent of "quit crying and get back in the game!"

Some pastoral leadership books and blog posts should come with a warning label: DO NOT ATTEMPT THIS

IF YOUR CHURCH IS NOT HEALTHY! It would save many hurting churches from piling on a load of extra and unnecessary grief.

So what are some of the ways in which a hurting church should be treated differently than a healthy one?

1. Do more hands-on pastoral care

So much of the current advice about pastoring feels like they're telling us how to pastor less, not more. I understand the sentiment behind much of that, and I've written extensively about the importance of what I call the Pastoral Prime Mandate, as seen in Ephesians 4:11–12. In that passage, the pastor is called to join hands with other church leaders (specifically, that passage names apostles, prophets, evangelists, and teachers), not to do all the ministry *for* church members, but "to equip God's people to do His work and build up the church, the body of Christ" (NLT).

"Every member a minister" is always the goal for a healthy church. But in hurting churches, hands-on pastoral care is more important, just like a hospital ICU has more doctors per patient than a standard hospital room. It's only when the patient becomes healthier that they receive less attention from health care professionals and start tending to their own care.

Before a pastor steps back from hands-on pastoral care, we need to ask a very important question: "Is the patient healthy enough for this yet?" I was a *very* hands-on pastor for many years. And I don't regret it, because I had inherited a very unhealthy, broken church and they needed a lot of attention for those first years.

Now I'm far less hands-on because part of the work I did during the hands-on season was to train others to do the work of ministry. Now the patient is healthy and does a much better job taking care of herself.

2. Make fewer demands on the congregation

Too many pastors think the answer for a broken church is to push people to do more. That may be the quickest way to kill an ailing congregation, especially when experiencing a crisis—or in the immediate aftermath of one.

There are a lot of very busy, very ill churches. It's foolhardy to add more ministries to a church that's struggling with their current ministries. No, don't coddle the church. But there are seasons when churches need rest more than they need exercise.

That happened in the first few years at my current church. They'd been through five pastors in ten years, each of whom brought new ideas and a new set of activities to go with them. The church was worn out from trying to please each pastor, so I gave them a rest. For a couple of years, we worshiped, taught Scripture, and hung out at picnics and potlucks. After a while, the patient got stronger and started standing, then walking on their own.

Today, I'm thrilled to pastor one of the strongest, most innovative and healthiest churches I know. But we wouldn't be here today if we hadn't slowed down for those years of much-needed, purposeful rest.

3. Alternate short bursts of activity with long periods of rest

Once a church starts becoming healthy, a wise pastor will protect them from the temptation to do too much, too soon. A church recovering from ill-health and broken-ness needs to be challenged. Then they need to rest. This helps them assess, heal, and prepare for the next challenge.

We have to help people stretch beyond their own comfort, but not so far that it will break them. Knowing just how far that is before giving them a break is another reason congregations need more hands-on pastoral care during these seasons.

I call this bungee-cord leadership. Here's how it goes: I try to imagine that there's a bungee cord or rubber band connecting us. If I'm not challenging them enough, the band stays limp and there's nothing to pull people. This produces passivity and ineffectiveness. But if I get out too far ahead of them, it can snap. This produces directionless churches and lonely, frustrated leaders.

Staying in the zone between too little and too much tension is one of the most challenging tasks a leader faces. Especially over a long period of time. Leaders need to keep just the right amount of tension to pull people forward, without allowing the cord between them to break.

Leaders who guide people through big events, crises, and changes have learned to leverage tension well. They've strengthened that cord and increased the congregation's tolerance for tension, allowing for consistent, healthy progress.

4. Fill them up before emptying them out

Of the five marks of a healthy church, some fill us up, others empty us out.

We fill up with: worship, fellowship, and discipleship.

We empty out with: discipleship, ministry, and evangelism.

Yes, discipleship is on both lists. It's the bridge that fills us up with knowledge and training, then it empties us out when we put it into practice.

A healthy church maintains an even balance of filling themselves up and emptying themselves out. A church that is emptying themselves in ministry may think they're healthy because they're busy. But unless they're also filling up with teaching, worship, and fellowship, they're as unhealthy as the church that keeps to themselves. We need to follow the example of Jesus who regularly pulled away from doing ministry to get refilled.

A healthy human body needs to fill up through nutrition and empty out through exercise. So does a healthy church. In the meantime, an unhealthy church may need a little more filling up before they have something to empty out.

This takes on new meaning after months of social isolation. While "filling up" in this context

STAYING IN THE ZONE BETWEEN TOO LITTLE AND TOO MUCH TENSION IS ONE OF THE MOST CHALLENGING TASKS A LEADER FACES

refers to receiving spiritual and emotional nourishment, it also has implications for getting back into our buildings again.

Reconvening for worship will not be like flipping a switch. It will be more like going to physical therapy after our muscles have atrophied. Doing previously "normal" church activities might feel awkward, even painful at times. Churches that were healthy before the lockdown might experience unexpected tension over how, when, and how quickly to open, how many people to allow in the building, whether or not to sing, and so on. Even the strongest churches must be allowed time to recover before any of this feels normal.

This season apart should always be a reminder of two contrasting but corresponding realities. First, that we don't need to be in our buildings to serve as the church. Second, that we can only stay apart for so long. Worshiping together is an essential element of the Christian life. We need each other's physical presence to receive the emotional and spiritual nourishment from which to serve.

CHURCH TURNAROUND IS
AN ATTITUDE, NOT AN EVENT

You can't program a church out of a crisis. No amount of special events, "Big Days," or new ideas can cause a broken church to become whole. There is no book, no conference, no blog post or podcast that will give you the key to church renewal or revival.

Sure, those things might give you the tools to attract a bigger crowd or generate more buzz, but church health isn't about more people or greater enthusiasm. It's about more of Jesus, His Great Commandment, and Great Commission.

Church turnarounds don't happen with slicker marketing or bigger offerings. They come slowly. Deliberately. Three steps forward, two steps back. Over a long period of time. Crowds can be built quickly. People heal slowly.

It starts with prayer and care. But those are slow processes. It takes a long time for people in a broken church to move from damaged to restored, from toxic to joyful, from distrust to surrender, from weak to strong, from hopeless to hopeful.

I've seen churches go from small to large in short periods of time. But I've never seen a shortcut to health and wholeness. As a pastor in a time of recovery, don't be in such a hurry to build a crowd that you forget about rebuilding the church. After all, anyone can draw a crowd. But only Jesus builds the church.

And, my fellow pastors, remember this: Sometimes the hardest and longest turnaround doesn't need to happen in the congregation, the leaders, or the worship team. The turnaround needs to happen in us first.

CROWDS CAN BE BUILT QUICKLY. PEOPLE HEAL SLOWLY.

Some of us need to remember why we became pastors in the first place, what our call was really all about—that it wasn't about programs, buildings, crowds, or status. It was about Jesus. And it needs to be again.

Find your first love. Grab on tight. And never let go. Turnaround starts at the foot of the cross.

CHURCH TURNAROUNDS ARE ABOUT DIRECTION AND CONSISTENCY, NOT SPEED OR SIZE

Church turnarounds are hard, but so rewarding.

When a church that was sick and dying goes through a

revitalization that puts them back on the path of effective mission, it's something we ought to celebrate and learn from. And it can act as a huge encouragement to other churches that are struggling, because it's evidence that they can turn around too.

Because we love stories told in big, broad strokes, the turnarounds we usually hear about are the ones that went "from thirty to three thousand in three years!" But it's important to guard ourselves against the expectation that such spectacular stories are the usual way church turn-arounds happen.

When we normalize excep-tional turnaround stories, we can unintentionally belittle and dis-courage those making consistent, steady progress. Most churches

TURNAROUND STARTS AT THE FOOT OF THE CROSS.

will work for three, four, or five years or longer with few visible results to show for it, even though a healthy turn-around is actually happening.

That's my story. Almost thirty years ago I was called to help a church turn around from a decade of numerical, emotional, spiritual, and missional decline. There were about thirty very discouraged people when I arrived and, while I wasn't expecting to go "from thirty to three thousand in three years!" I did expect a lot more than we got. The church is situated on a busy street in a very populated area, after all. Onward and upward, right?

If you had told me that the church would still be under one hundred and worshiping in the same small building after ten years of pastoring, I probably would not have taken the assignment. And if you'd told me that we'd be under two hundred and in the same building more than twenty-five years later (as in, today), I'd have been out the door so fast there'd be a Roadrunner cartoon trail of smoke behind me.

But here I am. In exactly that spot. And I'm so profoundly grateful to be here.

We always hear about the fast, big turnarounds. Those are great, but they're not typical. If your turnaround pace sounds more like my pace, that's normal. Keep at it. Church turnarounds are called turnarounds for a reason. They're more about the direction you're heading than the speed you're going.

Since slow and steady is normal, those who are doing it consistently should be recognized, resourced, encouraged, normalized, and celebrated.

CHAPTER 3

COMMUNICATION: RELAYING A FRESH VISION FOR THE FUTURE

Have you ever wondered why virtually every church leader is constantly writing and speaking about change? Including me?

Because we live in the fastest-changing culture ever. Change is not just an occasional reality. It's the water we're swimming in.

For instance, every time an app on your smartphone has an update, you're seeing a change that used to take at least a year to happen. In the pre-internet era, updates for your desktop computer were delivered annually on a disc that you bought in a box (containing a one-hundred-page instruction book) at your local store. Now they happen several times a week—or a day.

And now those changes have been turbocharged. In the global pandemic we've all experienced, it only took us a few days to learn how to livestream our church services, send video greetings with our phones, and get bored with videoconferences. The faster these changes happen, the more important it is to remember what doesn't change: the gospel of Jesus.

If we're not aware of how the world around us is changing, we'll miss out on an opportunity to share the gospel with that world. Not because the gospel will become irrelevant. Quite the opposite. The more everything else changes, the more important the good news of Jesus will be. But the way people hear, understand, and receive the timeless gospel is changing. Fast. If we don't realize and adapt to those changes, the people who need to hear it will be left on the sidelines—at least in part due to our stubbornness and ignorance.

People whose lives are constantly being upended by

change are desperate for a permanent rock they can cling to. That rock is the gospel of Jesus.

THE DIFFERENCE BETWEEN CHURCHES THAT ARE RESPONDING WELL AND THOSE THAT ARE NOT

Everyone's adapting now. But not all churches are adapting well. Based on everything I'm seeing, including hundreds of conversations with pastors and church leaders over the last few months, here are my three biggest pieces of advice for congregations attempting to survive and thrive in the midst of a global crisis:

1. Respond contextually

Over the last few months you may have had to scramble to figure out how to do church online. That's good. But that's not the best way to meet your congregation's or your neighbors' greatest needs.

So what are their greatest needs? And how can your church meet them? I don't know. Because I don't live and minister where you live and minister. But you do.

Your church, your neighborhood, and your town are not the same as someone else's church, neighborhood, or town. But most pastors—starting with me—don't know the world outside of our church walls as well as we should. We need to get offline and out of churches (or homes) for a while and take a look outside. What do your church members and your neighbors need? And how can you meet that need in a way that's specific to your context?

People can find generic help and advice anywhere. They need you to think and act contextually. Be present in your neighborhood.

2. Respond personally

The best ministry you will do if you're still in full or partial quarantine will be with the low-tech part of your high-tech phone. As in, making a lot of person-to-person phone calls. Let them hear your voice. Pray with them, cry with them, and laugh with them. Ask what they need, then have someone drop those groceries or that medicine off at their door.

The virtual church service that's working for the congregation down the street may or may not work for your church, so don't follow the lead of other churches. Follow the lead of the Holy Spirit and the needs of your congregation.

Then meet that need in the most personal way you can.

3. Prepare continually

This. Will. Happen. Again.

Maybe not a pandemic. But we live in a fallen world where bad things happen. Your church and community will be threatened with disaster again. The next time it may be a hurricane, an earthquake, a flood, or a fire. It's not a matter of *if* an emergency will arise, but *when*.

In this current crisis, the difference between churches that are struggling or closing and those that are alive and blessing others isn't their size, their budget, or even their faith. It's about their preparedness.

So what have they been doing that has set them apart from churches that aren't prepared? Based on my experience and conversations, three items keep coming up. The churches that are struggling or closing instead of stepping up and blessing their members and neighborhoods have:

1. No cash reserves
2. No team-based leadership
3. No adaptability

And that goes for some very big churches and ministries, not just small ones. Let's look at why each of those matters so much.

1. *Cash Reserves.* The first churches to fall were those who were already on the edge financially. Often carrying massive mortgages they should never have committed to in the first place.

Debt is the biggest church-killer in our lifetime. There are some very cutting-edge churches with big debt that won't make it through this crisis. Meanwhile, other churches that haven't seemed relevant for years are weathering it just fine because they have no debt. In fact, many of them are not just weathering it, they're able to step up and be a huge blessing to others because of their prior fiscal responsibility.

It's not a lack of faith that puts a plan in place and cash reserves in the bank. It's good stewardship. No, it's not easy. Especially in smaller churches that aren't even paying their pastor. But we're not called to do what's easy, we're called to do what's right.

After this storm has passed, prepare for the next one. Start putting small amounts of money away month by month. Create and train an emergency-preparedness team.

In fact, your church can be a gathering place where readiness classes can be taught and your neighbors *will* attend. Preparedness is not building bigger barns (Luke 12:13–21), it's counting the cost before you start (Luke 14:28).

2. *Team-Based Leadership.* Churches that rely on the pastor for everything are not adapting well. And many pastors who were already overworked are being pushed past their breaking points.

But churches with team-based leadership that uses everyone's gifts and talents, discipling new believers, and training new leaders—well, they're not just surviving, they're thriving in ways they never dreamed possible. I've heard from several pastors that some of their former pew-sitters are stepping up and helping out now that they're no longer able to sit in their pew.

> IT'S NOT A LACK OF FAITH THAT PUTS A PLAN IN PLACE AND CASH RESERVES IN THE BANK. IT'S GOOD STEWARDSHIP.

Right now, more than ever before in my lifetime, church members are asking, "How can we help?" In churches with team-based leadership, there's something for these new volunteers to do. In churches that rely on the pastor for everything, the response is often a shrug of the shoulders. The pastors literally don't know how to use the help that's being offered because there's no system in place for volunteers to step into.

3. *Adaptability.* Adaptable churches have pivoted in some big ways recently without losing much, or anything, in the process. But churches that are locked in on certain methods have not only suffered, many of them have closed their doors forever—and many more of them will close in the coming months and years.

Adaptability is not about abandoning biblical principles. Adaptability is what Jesus, the apostle Paul, and the early church did with such breathless ease it amazed everyone. Can't meet in the synagogue? Use a house. Can't meet in a house? Meet down by the river. Chased from Jerusalem because of persecution? Tell everyone about Jesus as you're running down the highway.

CHAPTER 4

PASTORAL CARE: MINISTERING TO PEOPLE AT VARIOUS STAGES OF GRIEF

In 1969, Elisabeth Kübler-Ross wrote the groundbreaking book *On Death and Dying*,[1] in which she laid out her theory that people face crisis by going through five stages of grief. These stages have become such a part of our lives and language that it's hard to imagine a time when we weren't aware of them. For instance, anytime anyone uses the phrase "you're in denial," they're citing Kübler-Ross—usually unintentionally.

As we work through this crisis and its aftermath, there will be people in your congregation who are at every one of these stages. Of course, that's always been the case, as everyone is experiencing different stages of crisis and grief in their personal lives. But in the COVID-19 aftermath, these stages will be far more pronounced.

SEEING THE STAGES OF GRIEF THROUGH A NEW LENS

According to Kübler-Ross, people process grief by walking through five distinct steps:

- Denial
- Anger
- Bargaining
- Depression
- Acceptance

Everyone goes at their own pace and some get stuck at one stage or another, but most people who arrive at a healthy emotional destination spend at least some time at each stage. What's different about leading people through a prolonged crisis like this is that there's always some new trauma to work through.

I'm noticing that these steps are manifesting in people's lives through two very distinct lenses:

Lens 1: The traditional manner of seeing these stages as a healthy way to process our grief. Each of the first four stages is a necessary but temporary step toward the healthy final stage.

Lens 2: A whole new way of seeing these stages as templates through which people see the world and interpret new data. When seen through Lens 2, these stages are not progressive steps as much as they are categories. I've noticed that each stage can be a helpful means to identify an individual's primary way of interpreting new events and traumas.

Here's a quick, crudely drawn description of how I use Lens 2 to recognize each of these stages as a camp that different church members will be living in. Since they're not steps toward a goal when seen through this lens, I've listed them alphabetically instead of progressively.

Acceptance: These are folks who are most likely to use phrases like "the new normal" and "it is what it is." They don't necessarily like it, but they accept it readily and want to adapt quickly.

Anger: There's a lot to be angry about. From lost loved ones, to poor political decisions, to bureaucratic red tape, you'll be pastoring some people who are responding to hurt with anger. They'll often use phrases like "if you're not angry, you're not paying attention!"

Bargaining: These are the fixers. People who think "if we just did this or that," we could make everything right again. They're often your best volunteers, but they may be burning themselves out trying to do too much.

Denial: These are folks who are more likely to point out the lies and falsehoods than the truths. They use phrases like "you can't trust anyone; they're all liars." They might even be convinced that, while the virus was/is real, everything around it was/is fake. Unfortunately, there's enough false information mixed in with the truth to validate this.

Depression: People may slip in and out of this stage at a moment's notice and without realizing it. They're likely to say things like "I just don't care anymore," meaning they care very deeply but they feel so hopeless that they wish they didn't care. This often feels like the end of the road but, thankfully, it doesn't have to be.

So, how does a pastor lead a church full of members who are not just working through these stages emotionally (Lens 1), but are using one of those stages as a way of interpreting new information (Lens 2)?

First, acknowledge your own feelings and tendencies. Using Lens 1, pastors and church leaders need to walk through these stages toward a healthy acceptance. Then, using Lens 2, we need to acknowledge our bias toward one or more stages as our primary interpretive tool. We can't help others if we won't acknowledge our own reality.

Second, keep moving. If you as a leader feel stuck at one stage (Lens 1), seek whatever help you need to move through all the stages to a place of healthy acceptance. (We'll see more on this issue of pastoral self-care later in chapter 5.)

Third, recognize their stage. We can't mentor someone in denial the same way we mentor someone in depression or anger.

Fourth, don't force the issue. While it's important to recognize where each person is so we can minister to them well, it's seldom helpful to show someone how vulnerable they are if they're not ready to accept it.

Fifth, don't pick sides. Telling someone their feelings are wrong is neither accurate nor helpful.

Sixth, help them identify their issues. Helping people know that what they're feeling is both normal and temporary helps them adapt better now, while anticipating and preparing for what's coming next.

Seventh, connect them. One of the blessings of being in a local congregation with people at all stages of grief is that those who got unstuck can help those who are currently stuck.

Eighth, be a pastoral presence. People working their way through the emotional stages of crisis and grief don't need answers as much as they need the reassuring presence of someone they know and trust.

CHAPTER 5

STAFF: ENCOURAGEMENT AND TEAM-BUILDING

This is harder than I expected.

All of it. From the lockdown to this weird middle ground, to whatever's coming next, the sense of constant uncertainty is wearing on me.

No, I'm not sick. And none of my loved ones are. For those of you who are sick or who are dealing with the illness or the death of a loved one, I cannot imagine your burden. But even for those of us who were simply asked to stay home, then walk through the phased steps to return to something close to normal, this is proving hard in some unexpected ways.

If you're in a position of leadership, your feelings may be very confusing right now. Even erratic. After all, we're used to knowing what to do. And we usually have a clear idea of how to help others know what to do. But not now. Even as I'm writing this book, I feel very unqualified to do so. Most days I feel more in need of comfort than qualified to give it.

Yet, at the same time as I'm working through my emotional issues, I feel a responsibility to lead. To help. To bless others. In fact, I don't just *feel* that responsibility, I *have* that responsibility.

SELF-CARE FOR LEADERS WHO ARE BARELY HOLDING ON

How do we lead others when each day feels like it runs past us in bits and pieces, and we're barely able to concentrate on anything for more than a few minutes at a time?

Give yourself a break.

Slow down.

Don't push.

Relax.

Stay healthy first.

It's okay if you don't have the answers right now. None of us have clear answers at the moment.

But we know the one who does. So lean on Jesus. Lean on each other. And let yourself grieve, mourn, or just feel *blah* for a while.

As I write this, we're in the third month of lockdown, and we're hearing there may be several months more of it in some form. So I have no idea where you (or I) will be when you read this. But here's how I'm feeling at the moment:

In the middle of a lockdown, during a pandemic, it's hard to remember what day it is. Without the usual markers, one day blends into the other in a confusing emotional haze. My sleep is off too. And with my sleep goes my ability to think and lead clearly.

You too? Yes, me too.

So how can we stay stable and sane in the middle of such uncertainty? Here are a few ideas that are especially helpful for pastors and other leaders:

1. Talk to yourself the way you'd talk to others

If a friend or church member told you they were mad at themselves for not being able to function at peak performance during a crisis, what would you tell them? To get over it? To work harder? To stop whining because people are depending on them?

I sure hope not.

I expect you'd go easy on them and help relieve their feelings of guilt. You'd sympathize. You'd emphasize their need to rest emotionally, physically, mentally, and spiritually. That's good advice. We need to talk to ourselves the same way.

2. Be vulnerable

There's nothing wrong with letting the people you lead know what you're feeling. In fact, it can create a sense of empathy and trust. I told you how I'm feeling for exactly that reason.

"But won't they have less respect for me if they see my weakness?" Not unless you're in a completely toxic environment. Chances are that your cracks are already being seen by the people who know you best—even over a video chat. Being honest about your challenges instead of working so hard to hide them might provide a great deal of relief for them too.

It's hard to believe we're in this together when the leader seems invincible—or, even worse, when you're obviously *not* invincible but are acting that way.

3. Embrace deeper truths

There are always two sets of truths running parallel in our lives—especially at a time like this.

Immediate truths: I feel confused, hurt, angry, or fearful right now.

Deeper truths: I know that God is greater than my current feelings, and I have faith that He'll get us through.

Both are true.

Although the immediate truths are more obvious and visceral, the deeper truths are more real. We need to acknowledge the immediate truths, but embrace the deeper truths.

"I'm feeling defeated right now, but I know God is able."

"My mind is in confusion, but my heart will follow Jesus."

"This feels scary, but greater is He who is in us than he who is in the world."

4. Lean on others

Pastors do too much alone. This has to change. And there's no better time than now to start making that change.

Now, more than ever, people understand their—and your—limitations. Not only is it okay to ask friends, family, and church members to help out, it's essential.

5. Invest in personal relationships

There's a big emphasis on technology right now. Understandably so. But the more we have to go virtual, the more valuable the personal touch will be. Even if that touch can't be physical, it matters more than ever that it's personal.

Regular "how are you doing?" phone calls are more important than ever. The "how can I help?" text is vital. And the follow-up with a box of groceries or an extended time to talk, pray, and cry is essential. Not just for them, but for you too.

6. Stay physically active

This is one I'm not doing as well as I should. Instead of accelerating the weight-loss regimen I was on, it's gone into reverse. This is not good. Not for my body, my emotions, or my spirit.

I understand why it's happening. Motivation is hard. And comfort food feels so good. But it's more important now than ever to stay healthy.

7. Get plenty of rest

As I mentioned earlier, my sleep patterns are off. So, I'm embracing the daily nap. If you can't sleep through the night, take a nap. If you can't nap, close your eyes and rest. We're all going through trauma right now. Trauma demands rest.

8. Practice spiritual disciplines outside of sermon prep

Pray, read the Scriptures, ponder—not to get sermon material, but to stay connected to Jesus.

9. Seek professional help

In severe situations, you may need to get outside assistance. Reach out to a mentor, a coach, a financial consultant, a therapist, or someone else who has more training than you do. It's not weakness to ask for help. It's weakness and foolishness—usually based in pride—not to use it when you need it.

10. Write it all down

There is no better way to find clarity in the middle of confusion than to write down what you're thinking, feeling, and wondering about. Even if you don't find answers as you write, the act of turning those ethereal feelings into something more tactile through your fingertips has a way of clearing the cobwebs.

WE'RE ALL GOING THROUGH TRAUMA RIGHT NOW. TRAUMA DEMANDS REST.

This will also give you a more accurate record of your thoughts, feelings, and actions that will serve you well as the days turn into weeks and possibly months.

11. Have some fun

Don't be so serious all the time. Laughter and joy are gifts from God—open them up and play with them.

HOW TO LEAD WHEN YOU'RE NOT FEELING LIKE A LEADER

It's hard to feel smart, brave, or faith-filled right now. Which means it's hard to lead others right now. But what do you do when you're in a position of leadership and you want to step up and lead, but you're not feeling smart, brave, or filled with faith?

Years ago, I read a quote that has helped me in so many moments of low faith, energy, and courage. I wish I could remember who wrote or said it so I could credit them. But here's my paraphrase of it:

> When I'm feeling smart and brave, I write everything down. I don't worry about details, grammar, or spelling. I just get it written down in list format. Then, when I'm not feeling smart or brave, I work the list. I edit the language. I schedule the meetings. In short, I do what I can. When I'm *not* feeling smart or brave, I work on the list I wrote when I *was* feeling smart and brave.

What does this look like in my own life? In this time of crisis, my moments of faith, courage, and insight are feeling fewer and fewer. So it matters more than ever that I don't squander them.

For me, I feel at my smartest, bravest, and most faith-filled in the morning. As the day moves on, I wear down. So I use my mornings to their best advantage. I write then. I ponder, I pray, I create. As much as I can, I don't schedule meetings for early mornings. I hold them later in the day.

As the day moves along and I feel less smart, creative, and faith-filled, I don't just give up. I work the list. I go back and see what I wrote that morning, then I follow through with the necessary meetings, editing, and whatever else is needed to move those ideas forward.

We're all in a similar place, to one degree or another. Our moments of faith, lucidity, and courage may be very rare. That makes them more valuable. Your highs and lows won't be the same as mine, but we all have them. And if we understand and use them well, we can leverage those rare, precious moments of faith, courage, and creativity for the glory of God and the blessing of others.

If we use our creative moments well, we can give ourselves plenty of productive tasks to do, even during the low-energy times. Then we can truly lead others, because we'll be allowing Jesus to lead us first.

CHAPTER 6

FINANCES: DEALING WITH A SHORTFALL

Churches have to do more ministry with less money. That's been true every year for the forty-plus years I've been in pastoral ministry, and this crisis has accelerated it.

So how can we keep doing all the ministry we need to do? Do we hire a firm to help us raise funds? Preach more about stewardship? Do more fundraising? More bake sales? Sell property? No. The absolute best way to solve our church's financial problems is so simple, so biblical, and so obvious it almost seems patronizing to state it.

The answer to poor finances is better discipleship. Because making disciples is always better than raising funds. When a church is making disciples, a whole lot of problems get smaller or go away entirely—including financial challenges. This happens because of a simple, logical, three-step reality.

- First, when church members are discipled, they do more ministry.
- Second, when church members do more ministry, the church needs less money.
- Third, when church members do more ministry, they give more generously.

Discipleship is not a magic pill. If we use it as a fundraising scheme, we'll be abusing its intent and be disappointed in the results. But when we see it the way it was intended—as the central focus of the pastor's calling and an essential aspect of the church's mandate—it will raise the level of everything we do as a church. Including helping us to do a lot more ministry with far less money.

Plus, discipleship is a much healthier way for a church to function anyway. With more members contributing of their time, gifts, and talents, instead of simply dropping money in the plate and expecting paid staff to take care of them, the entire church becomes healthier and more effective.

Jesus actually gave us very few commands. But one of the greatest (in fact, the only one repeated in all four gospels and the book of Acts) is the command to make disciples.

Our churches can face the current financial crunch in one of two ways: see it as a problem that requires us to squeeze more money out of people, or see it as an opportunity to take discipleship more seriously. If we see it as an opportunity and redouble our efforts

THE ANSWER TO POOR FINANCES IS BETTER DISCIPLESHIP. BECAUSE MAKING DISCIPLES IS ALWAYS BETTER THAN RAISING FUNDS.

to make disciples, not only will our financial problems be fewer, but our churches will get healthier, our members will grow in Christ, and our kingdom impact will increase.

THE TWO BIGGEST MISTAKES CHURCHES MAKE WITH MONEY

There are two equal but opposite mistakes churches regularly make regarding money. These are the main ways that finances (or lack of them) sometimes stop us from doing the ministry we're called to do.

Mistake #1: Giving veto power to the accountant, treasurer, or budget.

Mistake #2: Ignoring the accountant, treasurer, or budget.

Let's look at Mistake #1 first.

So many good congregations want to do great ministry, but their limited finances cause them to make too many decisions based on what they can or can't afford instead of what God is calling them to do. It's a trap that may seem impossible to get out of. But there is hope. Our church discovered this hope over two decades ago when we made a decision that has been a great starting point in allowing us to follow God more and money less.

It's so simple I can't believe we didn't see it all along. Our church makes all our ministry decisions based on the mission, not on our financial ability.

Churches should never make ministry decisions based

on what we can afford for two primary reasons. First, because if we pencil it out in advance, there will always be a reason we can't afford it. Second, because prioritizing the budget puts money (a.k.a. "mammon," Matt. 6:24 KJV) in charge of the church instead of the mission. We can no longer allow money to make decisions for the church. The mission must lead.

Ask yourself this question: What is God calling our church to do? Open a food bank? Be an evangelistic center? Support missions? Plant other churches? Then do it!

You don't have enough money to do it? Do it anyway, by starting with the parts that don't require finances:

- Pray
- Assemble a team
- Do research
- Look for strategic partners
- Use the currency of time (more on that later)
- Put a work day on the calendar

Start small, if you must. But, by all means, start! Never give money the power over whether or not to do any ministry. Just figure out how to do it in a way that is financially responsible and feasible—what the Bible calls good stewardship.

Now, let's address Mistake #2. While we can't give veto power to the accountant, treasurer, or budget, we can't ignore them either.

OUR CHURCH MAKES ALL OUR MINISTRY DECISIONS BASED ON THE MISSION, NOT ON OUR FINANCIAL ABILITY.

When our church decided we would never let money be the deciding factor of whether or not to do a ministry, that didn't mean we stopped paying attention to the financial bottom line. Instead, we use it as one of many factors to determine *how* we'll do the ministry we know we're called to do, including the availability and skills of our volunteers, the size of the need, and so on. Our church's financial reality is never ignored, but it's never in charge.

By making money one aspect of many in our "how to" list, we've never had to say no to any ministry we knew we were supposed to do. Sometimes we find a way to do it without money, and sometimes the money comes in after we get going, since God always provides the means for His mission. But ministry always comes first.

THE FAST-CHANGING
LANDSCAPE OF CHURCH GIVING

The way people give is changing. And this crisis has accelerated those changes.

The good news: everyone is experiencing this, so you're not alone in it. The bad news: everyone is experiencing this, so even the usual lifeboats (denominational support and so on) are less likely to be there when we need them.

Since these changes in church giving patterns are so universal, the sooner we understand and adapt to what's happening, the better. Let's take a look at some major shifts in the way people give to their local church:

1. Time is the new church currency

One of the biggest changes churches need to make in the next few decades is to move away from an offering-based church economy toward a time-based church economy.

While the bad news is that there's less money available, the good news is that today's givers are ready to get their hands dirty. They're not less generous than previous generations, they're just less likely to want to pay someone else to do ministry on their behalf. Unfortunately, most of our church systems are set up to utilize people's money more than their time. We want donors more than volunteers. Givers more than workers.

Time, not money, is the new church commitment currency. We need to adapt the way we do church to show people that their time is valuable to us. But we've structured our churches on a money-based system for too long. We're going to lose a lot of churches that can't make the transition.

It's essential to help people get as much value as possible for both their time and their money. Starting on time, being prepared, and ending when promised doesn't just matter for the occasional attender, it matters for the hard-working volunteer even more. Churches that make people wait while they get their act together will lose them faster than ever. And they'll lose highly motivated people the fastest of all.

2. More work teams, fewer committees

Teams do things. Committees tell others to do things—including deciding where the money will go. Today's givers want to put their time and money into ministry teams rather than serve on a committee. And they don't want members of an uninvolved committee standing in judgment over what their team does with their time and money.

3. Give them an experience they can't get online

People used to come to church for a great sermon. That's still high on their list[1] for choosing one church over another, but if that's all the value they're getting, they can and will continue to stay home and watch online—and not necessarily their home church.

When people go through the trouble of leaving their house to attend church (when they *can* attend church, that is), what they experience in person needs to be better than what they can get online.

TIME, NOT MONEY, IS THE NEW CHURCH COMMITMENT CURRENCY.

We have to pay as much attention to opportunities for passionate worship, deep friendship, and meaningful service as we do to a well-crafted sermon.

4. Challenge them to commit, not just to donate

People need to know that when we talk about giving, it's more than just finances. Generous people give more than their money. They need opportunities to offer their time, experience, and talents in ways that spur a generosity of spirit.

5. Don't be the only recipient of their generosity

Generous people want to attend and serve generous churches. Generous churches don't keep everything for themselves. Instead of everything landing at the church doorstep, we need to work with our church members to bless others in ways that don't have an obvious benefit to the church's bottom line.

Generous people are givers. And generous churches are too.

HOW TO REVERSE A DOWNWARD GIVING TREND IN AN OTHERWISE HEALTHY CHURCH

"Just preach the gospel and the money will take care of itself." That's been a popular phrase for as long as I can remember. Wouldn't it be great if it were true? But it's not. In even the healthiest and strongest of churches and ministries, finances are never automatic.

Here are some of the steps our church has discovered

by trial and error in the last couple of years that have helped us slow down, then reverse a downward giving trend in our church:

1. Emphasize generosity, not just giving

Giving is like any other skill. Very few people are born with an inbred desire and ability to give. Everyone needs to be taught how and why giving matters. And that's up to us, pastors. Thankfully, the Bible is full of great teaching about stewardship and generosity, but we must always remember that God's

GENEROUS PEOPLE WANT TO ATTEND AND SERVE GENEROUS CHURCHES.

Word is not as concerned with our money as with our hearts. Which is why we need to teach more about generosity than giving.

It's possible to give without being generous, but no one can be generous without giving. The size of the heart matters more than the size of the gift. If Jesus' teachings about generosity tell us anything, they tell us that.

2. Teach stewardship, not just giving

Our financial teaching cannot be all about trying to get more money out of people's pockets. That always ends badly because that's not what generosity is about. But as pastors, we have an obligation to God and the church to teach a balanced, biblical view of stewardship, not just giving.

In general, people want to be generous. Church members want to support the church ministries financially. What's stopping them isn't a lack of desire, but a lack of ability. They want to give, but they don't know how to do it without taking an already paper-thin financial margin and breaking it totally. Biblical stewardship gives them those tools.

3. Assume good intentions

We need to start with the assumption that the people who are regular church members are doing so voluntarily. They want the church and its ministries to succeed, and they'd like to know how they can help that happen.

When I mention our church's financial needs, I'll often use a phrase like "this is not about guilting anyone into giving. I'm assuming you're a part of this church because you *want* to help, so I'm letting you know about one of the ways you *can* help, if you're able."

4. Teach them how the church is funded

Facebook is free to its users. So are Google, YouTube, Instagram, and Pinterest. A couple of decades ago it would have been unimaginable to have such amazing tools, games, and entertainment at our disposal for free. But today, we're so used to it that we don't even pause to think about how they get paid for. Since we also receive most or all of the services of the local church for free, many new believers don't think about how the church's bills get paid any more than you spend thinking about how you get email for free.

Apps and websites pay for themselves through advertising, of course. But most churches rely entirely on donations. But many folks, especially new believers, may not know this. I've had several recent conversations with new believers who thought that when the church passes the plate, it's like the public school having a bake sale. They think there's some unknown entity paying the main bills, while the money they give is for extras.

We can't assume anything anymore. New believers need to be informed of the church's financial realities and their biblical responsibilities.

5. *Practice good stewardship of what is given*

People are less likely to donate to a church that isn't demonstrating good stewardship of what they give. For most churches and pastors, poor stewardship is not a matter of extravagance, but of unseen waste.

Over the last few years, our church has taken a hard look at all our expenses, and we found we were wasting money without knowing it. Here are just a few of the ways we've saved money, along with a few ideas other churches have used.

- *Share a copier lease with other churches or ministries:* We share a machine and its expenses with our preschool.
- *Talk to your power company:* A few years ago, our local power company replaced every light in our building with energy-efficient bulbs for free, including many of the fixtures. Then they supplemented the cost of replacing single-pane windows with energy-efficient (and much nicer-looking) double-pane windows. Many, maybe most, of your power companies have similar offers.
- *Go low- or no-maintenance on landscaping:* For us, in drought-stricken California, that meant replacing our real grass with fake grass.

- *Lose your "desktop" phones:* With cellphones, we haven't used them for anything but incoming calls for years anyway.
- *Share or rent your facility, if you have one:* Don't be in a hurry to buy a facility if you don't have one.

6. Hold special giving celebrations

New generations are less likely to give in a steady stream, and more likely to give in single doses. So let's provide opportunities that match the way they are most likely to give.

In addition to asking for monthly pledges for missions, facility upgrades, and so on, we've added two Sundays every year to take a special offering for those needs. We call them *Heart for the House Sunday* (a special offering for facility maintenance and upgrades) and *Heart for the World Sunday* (for missions and outreach).

Doing these special days has almost doubled what we receive in a given year for these projects. And when church members see a facility upgrade or hear about a ministry need that was met, they're more excited to give the next time.

7. Give quarterly updates

I used to only talk about the church budget once a year at the annual membership meeting. But by then the year had passed. We debated having a weekly or monthly bulletin update, but rejected that for our church for two reasons: 1) it was too often, and 2) it was better coming from the pastor's voice than reading it as a cold number on paper.

So what we do now is take a minute or two on a Sunday four times a year to bring them up to date. After sharing where we are compared to our anticipated budget, we always see a giving spike. People want to give when their gifts can be helpful. Sharing the need before the year ends allows them to do this.

8. Break down the need into doable bites

A few years ago our church came in at $8,000 under our expected annual income. That's a lot of money for a small congregation.

So, for the following year's budget, I broke it down for the congregation this way. At an average attendance of 150 people per Sunday, that $8,000 shortfall could have disappeared if every attender had given just $1 more each week ($150 x 52 = $7,800). If our church averaged 75 people, it would have meant $2 more per Sunday, and so on.

Obviously, not everyone is going to give exactly $1 every week, but when the need is broken down that way, people can see that every extra dollar they give adds up to a significant impact.

ONE SIMPLE STEP
TO CREATE A YEAR-END
GIVING BUMP IN YOUR CHURCH

A lot of churches get a nice year-end bump in their finances. During the Christmas season, even casual attenders come to church more often, churches hold annual events like Christmas bazaars that bring in funds, and the week of Christmas often attracts huge crowds—and offerings to match.

But not all churches experience this. Many churches (like every one I've ever pastored) either stay flat or they experience a financial downturn at the end of the year. Because of this, several years ago I discovered a simple idea that helps our church members plan their giving better, and it gives our church finances a healthy year-end bump.

In late autumn we send out a short letter to every regular giver with a "thank you" for their faithfulness and a record of what they've given so far. This simple practice is a great way to thank everyone for their generosity, while providing a helpful reminder before it's too late to make up for any unintentional shortfall for the calendar year.

WHAT'S IN THE LETTER?

So, what does this letter look like? It's simple.

First, the treasurer or bookkeeper uses the church's financial software to print up a copy of their giving for the year to date. Then a separate cover letter is added to the mailer.

Here's an example of a cover letter we've used:

_____ *(date)*

Hello (recipient's name),

As the calendar year draws to a close, I want to take a moment to thank you for your faithfulness in giving to the ministries of (church name) this year.

The Lord did so much in our church body in (year), and your faithfulness—including your financial giving—has contributed to that. We are truly grateful.

Also, we have found that this is a good time of the year to assess where we are. And our giving is one of those important areas to keep track of. So we've attached your record of giving to (church name) for this year so far. This is not a request for money, and we're not billing you for anything. It's just our copy of your giving, so you can compare it to your records.

By sending this out with several weeks still left in the year, everyone gets a chance to work out any differences between our records and your records now, rather than waiting until next year when everyone is under the strain of tax preparation.

And yes, we will still be sending you a giving record for all of (this year) at the beginning of (next year).

So take a look at your banking records, compare it to this record, then call (contact name and info) if your record doesn't match ours. We'll get to work on making it right for you.

Thanks again for your faithfulness in giving,
(Name and signature)

I highly recommend sending this notice old-school. By the post office. Snail mail, not email. There's something about the physical paper in their hand that gives this letter the feeling of importance that it deserves.

It makes the thank you feel as sincere as it actually is, and it makes it far more likely that the letter will actually be opened and read by the recipient.

We don't do ministry for the money—at least we shouldn't.

But this simple step is a good way to make sure our financial obligations get met, our church members get thanked, and our church records stay up-to-date.

Any time we can do all of that so simply and easily, we should take full advantage of it.

CHAPTER 7

TECHNOLOGY: REWORKING YOUR CHURCH'S ONLINE STRATEGY

Did anyone else get tired of doing church online as quickly as I did?

At first, I was grateful for the chance to continue meeting virtually even when we couldn't meet in real life. I was in awe of our church's creative team for the amazing work they did—especially on such short notice. And I was excited about the new opportunities to share the gospel in a different format.

But it didn't take more than a couple Sundays for the novelty to wear off. Soon, I wasn't just tired of watching church online, I was dreading the experience. While I remained grateful for the technology that allowed us to communicate when we weren't able to gather, online church didn't just feel less-than to me, it felt . . . I don't know . . . exhausting. Nothing will ever be able to replace the in-person church experience.

SCARCITY CREATES VALUE: WHY IN-PERSON CHURCH MATTERS EVEN MORE NOW

There's been a lot of talk about how the time has come for online church to finally be taken seriously. And I agree. If this recent crisis doesn't prove the need for it, nothing ever will. We need to do online church better. But one of the biggest lessons we need to take from this moment is clear: the rise of online church, as important as it is, shows us how precious the in-person church experience truly is.

Scarcity creates value. It's a basic rule of economics, relationships, and life. When we have a lot of something, the value attached to it goes down. When it's rare, its value goes up.

This will be true for the flesh-and-blood in-person church experience as we go forward. And not just in the church building. As we reach more people with an online church experience, the value of the in-person experiences of worship, fellowship, ministry, discipleship, and evangelism will increase exponentially.

The more online church grows, the more the personal touch will matter. We need to work just as hard at doing one as we do at the other.

IS ONLINE CHURCH *REAL* CHURCH?

The church needs to be more digital. But church will never be entirely digital. Screen-to-screen is no substitute for face-to-face. Digital reality cannot replace *actual* reality.

I've heard people complain that online church isn't *real* church. I disagree. Online church is *real* church for a lot of people. Especially for those who are restricted from attending church IRL (In Real Life) because of medical issues, geography, work schedules, and now a pandemic we never saw coming. Online church is *real* church, but it's not *enough* church.

There are some aspects of church that we can get online,

like teaching, worship, even conversation. Some churches have online pastors who are available to answer questions, receive prayer requests, and lead people to Christ. That's *real* church!

But there are a lot of aspects of a full church experience that require flesh-and-blood people to actually hang out in the same physical space together. From receiving communion, to laying on hands for prayer, to working out our conflicts, a full church experience requires our physical, human presence.

ONLINE CHURCH IS *REAL* CHURCH, BUT IT'S NOT *ENOUGH* CHURCH.

We need to do it safely, so it will look very different for a while, but I will never take the value of in-person church lightly ever again.

SO YOUR SMALL CHURCH LIVESTREAM STINKS—HERE'S WHY THAT'S OKAY

Just about every church is livestreaming their services now. Necessity being the mother of invention (and adaptation), we're all doing what we have to do.

Churches with preexisting livestream technology are learning how to conduct their service from an empty room, while those who haven't livestreamed before are learning the basics—fast.

But let's face two facts about churches that are new to the livestream world:

1. Most first-time streamers are my friends in small churches.
2. Most of us aren't doing livestream very well.

But that's okay. Here's why. You can't livestream your most-needed ministries. While it's important to make a Sunday experience available to your church members, a high-quality livestream Sunday service is not the most significant way you can serve your church or your community.

Top-notch video production is not what the typical small congregation expects or needs from their church leaders. Especially now. They need to hear from their pastor, their Sunday school teacher, and their friends. And not just on Sunday morning.

Every church needs to lean in to what they do best. If your service is being livestreamed (which I highly recommend), do it as best you can, but keep it simple. Then move on to doing the kinds of ministry you do well. Those kinds of small, simple, low-tech ministries will be of far greater value than how you frame a video shot.

At some time in the hopefully not-too-distant future, we'll be able to gather everyone in our church buildings all at the same time again. When that happens, we need to keep using the livestream option.

In years to come when people look back at this time, they won't be thinking about the quality of our livestream. They'll remember the personal "how are you doing?" text, the grocery drop-off, and the time their pastor or church friend stayed on the phone to pray with them through their fears and worries.

If you want to make a real difference, don't get bogged down in the details of video streaming. Focus on Jesus. Connect with the community. And invest in people more than technology.

THE WEIGHT OF TECHNOLOGY: HOW TO USE IT WITHOUT BEING OVERWHELMED BY IT

For larger churches, the switch to online services was unusual, but not especially difficult. After all, most midsize to large churches were already offering an online experience to correspond with their in-person church service. All they had to do was tweak a few things—and most did it really well.

But in the typical smaller church—which comprises up to 90 percent of all congregations, serving half of all church attenders—their online presence was minimal or nonexistent. Overnight, pastors who had no online experience and little or no technical expertise were stuck at home trying to figure out how to communicate with their church members in ways they'd never done before.

The same technology that is a boost to the ministry of midsize to large churches feels like a 100-pound weight on the shoulders of the typical small-church pastor. If that's you, here are a few simple steps to help you either get online or make your online presence better, without overwhelming you.

1. Use the best device(s) you already have

Most of the smartphones and laptops we're currently using are more than adequate to do the job. Plus, you already have some familiarity with them.

2. Be heard

If you have a mic that can plug into your device, use that. If not, use your earbuds. If not, the built-in mic on your device will do what you need.

3. Get close

If you're using the built-in mic on your device, you need to get as close as you can for the audio to be clear. But even if you're using an external mic, the biggest mistake I see most small churches making is that the camera is too far away from the speaker.

If you typically speak while standing still, you can get as close as a head-to-waist shot. If you move more, give the camera just enough distance to catch you where you typically move, then put tape on the floor so you know how far you can go while remaining in the frame.

4. Shoot in landscape (horizontal, not vertical)

Unless you're shooting in a format that demands a vertical (portrait) shot—like Instagram Stories—hold the phone wide, not tall. Otherwise, everyone who watches you on a laptop or TV will see you on less than a third of their frame.

5. Hold it still

Use a tripod if you have one. Unless it's a quick promotional video that you're shooting as a selfie, it needs to be stationary.

6. Shoot from above or even level with head

The shot from below is a combination of unflattering, intimidating, and awkward. But when you're shooting with the camera just above your head, it literally and figuratively lifts you—and therefore the viewer—up.

7. Light in front

If you're shooting in a room with a window, make sure it's in front of you, not behind you.

8. Look at the audience or the camera, not yourself

If you're speaking to a group, set the camera, then forget it. If you're speaking directly to the camera, find the camera lens (that irritating little dot) and look at that, not at the screen.

9. Keep it short

Unless you're simply livestreaming your existing in-person church service, video presentations should be shorter than in-person presentations. When people leave their home for an event, they expect you to go long enough to make it feel like it was worth leaving their home for. But when people are online, their attention spans are much shorter.

10. Review it

Unless your video is being livestreamed, it's essential to review it before sending it out. It's amazing how many times I've seen a video with a mistake so obvious that I've wondered aloud, "Did they even watch it before they sent it?"

11. Trim it

Most smartphones and laptops have simple, easy-to-learn apps that can help you trim the front and back of a video that otherwise flows as if it were happening live. If you don't know how to edit a video, that's okay. Do it "live," but be ready to stop and start fast. A quick reach up to start and stop is okay, but don't hit start, run to your seat, then get out of your seat to hit stop. If people see no one on the screen for even a second or two because you're running to get in front of the camera, you'll lose them.

12. Upload it

Like cameras, high-quality video platforms are everywhere. Use the one you're most familiar with. Facebook and YouTube are your best options since they're used by the most people and are easiest for people without a lot of technical expertise (or cost). It's easy to upload to them, and most of your audience is already familiar with how to use them.

13. Follow-up

If you're using livesstream, it's very helpful to let people know you'll be available afterward to engage with them. If you're prerecording your video, you can set a premiere time (this works best on YouTube). Then you can be online watching and answering questions before, during, and after the video is running. Then, after it's premiered, check back regularly or set an alert so you can respond to the comments of people who watch it later. This personal response can make up for many technical deficiencies.

THE ONLINE ON-RAMP

At best, a church's online presence is an on-ramp. The most important one we have right now and for the foreseeable future, for sure. But an on-ramp is not the endgame.

Discipleship is a long, multi-step process. If an online experience starts someone on that road, that's great! If we use the online experience as a first step toward fully engaged discipleship, it will have served a noble purpose. But if all we do is count eyeballs like we counted attendance, it will be a step backwards.

At some point—as soon as we're able—that online experience must translate into real-life, flesh-and-blood, in-person, disciple-making reality. When we do that, we'll have some success worth measuring.

CHAPTER 8

CLOSING A CONGREGATION: PROACTIVE OPTIONS FOR DYING CHURCHES

The church will last forever. Jesus promised that. But that doesn't apply to individual congregations. History shows us that congregations have a finite life span. This is a hard subject to talk about. But we can't ignore it. More congregations will close their doors permanently in the next couple of years than we've ever seen before.

Thankfully, many of those shuttered churches will be replaced by church plants, restarts, and so on. But even so, when a congregation closes its doors we need to do it well. The decisions about how to come to the end of a church's life span need to start long before the final "sold" sign is on the lawn. Unfortunately, we have not been doing this well. We need to downsize better.

This is a delicate, complex, multi-layered subject that could be the subject of a lengthy book on its own, but for now I want to focus on just one area that we could be making much better decisions in. Namely, what to do with the physical assets (mainly the land and building) of a dying church.

WHAT NOT TO DO

There are three mistakes I constantly see being made by dying churches when it comes to property management.

First, the slow fade. Some call it faith. Some call it hopefulness. I call it denial. Everyone can see that the church is dying. But no one is doing what needs to be done. For years the congregation may have been experiencing a slow fade in attendance, giving, and passion, but this crisis has accelerated those problems and now the unthinkable has become inevitable.

Too many churches have lost their facilities along with their congregations because they won't accept the reality that the congregation is at the end of its life span.

Second, the multiple mortgages. By the time a church needs to take on a second or third mortgage simply to pay the bills, the writing is on the wall. I'm sure there is some story of a dying church that leveraged the money from a second or third mortgage to buy extra time to figure out how to turn their congregation around, but I've never seen it.

MORE CONGREGATIONS WILL CLOSE THEIR DOORS PERMANENTLY IN THE NEXT COUPLE OF YEARS THAN WE'VE EVER SEEN BEFORE.

Third, the piece-by-piece sell-off. As with a mortgage, I've never seen a church sell off a portion of their land to pay bills, then keep the church alive beyond how long the money from the sale holds out. If your church has to mortgage the property or sell off pieces of it to pay the regular bills, you're at the point of no return.

There are better options. They're not easy. Some of you may not like me after reading some of them. But they're better than the inevitable loss of the church and all of its assets.

1. Give the property to a healthy, thriving church that needs it

Yep, just give it away.

Before loading a dying congregation down with (more) debt, before selling off so many chunks that what remains isn't worth much, find a healthy, thriving congregation or other ministry and give it to them.

Keep it in God's kingdom work. Instead of watching your property get chiseled away, sold by the bank, torn down, and turned into condos or a mini-mall, you can participate in the joy of seeing it supercharge a healthy but needy ministry.

2. Sell the property and donate the proceeds

In many situations, the church property is no longer in an ideal ministry location, but is well-suited for other purposes. If so, the best course of action may be to sell the property to whomever will pay top dollar, then donate the money to effective ministries that can carry on a portion of the church's mission and passion.

3. Sell the property to another ministry at a huge discount

If you can't give the property away for some reason (debt payments, denominational restrictions, and so on), sell it to another church or ministry for as little as you can. Near where I live, Teen Challenge owns a castle[1] for exactly this reason (yes, an actual castle—in California!). The castle was built in 1919. After passing through a couple of owners, it was bought by a Christian ministry. When they could no longer use it, they sold it to Teen Challenge (the best Christ-based recovery ministry I know of) for a massive discount off its market value.

Instead of being sold or lost to a bank, it has been used for decades to help change thousands of lives through the power of Jesus.

4. Invite other ministries to share the use (and the bills) of your property

When you find other churches or ministries that can use your property during your empty hours, they get a blessing, your church gets help paying the bills, and the property gets used for more ministry.

Plus, after working with them it can become a natural

launch-point for giving the property away to a ministry that your church members already know and love.

5. Partner with another church as a multisite campus

If your reaction to multisite is to bristle about it being a "takeover" by another bigger church, I have three responses:

First, I understand. I've seen some predatory behavior in this arena too.

Second, it doesn't have to be predatory. Plenty of multisite churches are truly collaborative. And many are happening from the partnership of small and midsize churches, not just one big church consuming the others.

Third, even if it is a church takeover, how is being taken over by another church worse than being taken over by the bank? As long as the church is doing good kingdom work, we should be grateful that a strong church is using our former property, even if they do it differently than we did.

This is not the old-school church merger in which two dying churches try to salvage what they have left. That just prolongs the deaths of both. For a church partnership to work, at least one of the congregations must be strong and thriving.

If there's a multisite church anywhere near you or within your network or denomination, sit down and talk with them before refusing to consider it. There may be a lot more good news there than you realize.

6. Close your church and give the building to a new church plant

Yes, there will be a lot of churches closing their doors in the next few years. But there will also be a lot of new churches starting up. Probably not enough to make up for the closures, but we can increase their odds of survival by helping them with one of the hardest aspects of a church plant—a place to meet.

CONGREGATIONS MAY DIE, BUT THE CHURCH NEVER WILL. THAT'S WHAT WE NEED TO INVEST IN.

A dying church that has done good work for the kingdom of God deserves more than to be forgotten or sold off piece by piece. If its hard-won assets can be kept in Christ's church, we have an obligation to do so.

I have a marker on my driver's license that says I'm an organ donor. If my body parts can be used to bring life to someone else when I'm done using them, I'm more than happy to do that. Our churches should do no less.

Just as my identity is not in my body, a church's identity is not in its building—or it shouldn't be. The building is a shell, a home, a vehicle. If it can be used by another church or ministry under another name, we should be thrilled to help that happen.

Congregations may die, but the church never will. That's what we need to invest in.

CHAPTER 9

NEXT: PREPARING YOUR CHURCH FOR WHAT'S COMING

Doing new things is scary. For some. Doing new things is exciting. For others.

But even if you fall more into the second category than the first (as I do), doing something new is always exhausting. And it's more exhausting when you're attempting to change something you've been doing for a long time. Which is why change gets harder as you get older.

And when you add the changes imposed upon us

because of a worldwide pandemic and its aftermath . . . nothing about this is easy.

CHANGE IS EXHAUSTING— DON'T ATTEMPT IT WITHOUT A WAY TO RECHARGE

Even if you know change needs to happen and everyone is on board with it, never underestimate how exhausting change is going to be—and how much that exhaustion will slow people down, make them second-guess themselves, or even want to abandon the entire process midstream. Including you.

This is why, whenever you're attempting a big change, it is essential to build intentional time and space for rest. The best way I know to do that is to decide in advance what long-term aspects you will never change, then utilize those permanent markers as your support system to help you tackle what needs to be changed.

Find places you can rest, like relationships, core theology, foundational traditions, and so on.

I've discovered this recently in my own life and ministry. I just turned sixty. In my fifties, I experienced a complete upheaval in the way I worship, minister, and work. In fact, it was more change than I've experienced in any previous decade—including the decade I started in ministry, got married, and had kids.

Some of those changes were planned. Some were not. Most of it has been good. And I've decided to embrace all of it.

But. It's. Exhausting.

And more is on its way.

This has made me more appreciative than ever of the things in my life that are as solid as a rock. Places I can go emotionally, spiritually, physically, and relationally to rest, relax, and recover. For me, this includes a twenty-seven-plus-year pastoral tenure with the great folks at Cornerstone, and an immediate and extended family who all live close by. But it also includes what it should include for all of us. An ongoing, deepening relationship with Jesus. The richness and depth of Scripture. The haven of prayer. Time away to ponder and reflect.

Change is necessary. It's essential for faith, growth, leadership, and life. But, even if you love it, don't ever let yourself step into places of great change without having the safety, security, and support of a place and a people where you can rest your head, heart, and spirit.

The more everything changes, the more important it is to have places to rest, find reassurance, and build up the courage to step out in faith again.

WHEN THIS IS OVER, LET'S BE SURE WE'VE LIVED STORIES WORTH TELLING

Crises have a way of bringing out both the best and the worst in us.

In the aftermath of 9/11, for instance, we heard stories of kindness, generosity, courage, and sacrifice that illustrated how the best of humanity outweighed the worst.

So far, in this pandemic, there's been a glut of stories showing the worst of us. From hoarding, to panic, to price-gouging, and more. But there are great things happening as well.

When I call so many of our homebound church members, they tell me they've been getting regular calls of encouragement and offers of assistance from other church members. Our young people are checking in on elderly neighbors and church members to ask if they can make a grocery run for them.

Health care workers and other essential businesses are working sacrificially. Neighbors are making their resources available at no cost. These stories need to be told more than the negative ones.

Wherever you live, whatever your circumstance, find a way you can bless someone else. When all this is over and we assess the results, those stories will be what we cling to.

Let's make sure we're all living in such a way that when the stories of this time are told, the ones that come from our lives and our churches will be stories we want people to hear. Stories that bless people, inspire hope, and honor Christ.

AFTERWORD

To write this book, I culled through more than one thousand articles that I wrote for church leaders over the last seven years. From those, I found about 150 that apply in times of crisis.

I edited and updated the material from about fifty of those articles for this book. I also added some new content (about thirty percent of the book) written during the first few months of the COVID-19 lockdown.

The result is the fastest book I've ever written because the need is so immediate. But the information is not knee-jerk. It's based on over forty years of pastoral experience, including leading a church through several crises and turnarounds. In addition, I've spent almost a decade teaching and writing for small-church pastors, and in the last few months, I've had innumerable conversations with pastors and other church leaders as we've faced this crisis together.

Through this process, I've discovered a handful of essential truths that will guide me through the coming months and years. I've presented them here in the hope they can help you and the church you serve too.

— KARL VATERS

NOTES

Chapter 1: Impact: What We Know—and What We Don't Know

1. David Haskel, "Liberal Churches Are Dying. But Conservative Churches Are Thriving," *The Washington Post*, Jan. 4, 2017, https://www.washingtonpost.com/posteverything/wp/2017/01/04/liberal-churches-are-dying-but-conservative-churches-are-thriving/.

Chapter 4: Pastoral Care: Ministering to People at Various Stages of Grief

1. Elisabeth Kübler-Ross, *On Death & Dying: What the Dying Have to Teach Doctors, Nurses, Clergy & Their Own Families* (New York: Simon & Schuster, 2014).

Chapter 6: Finances: Dealing with a Shortfall

1. "Why Americans Go (and Don't Go) to Religious Services," Pew Research Center, August, 1 2018, https://www.pewforum.org/2018/08/01/why-americans-go-to-religious-services/.

Chapter 8: Closing a Congregation: Proactive Options for Dying Churches

1. "Inland Empire Teen Challenge," Teen Challenge International, https://www.teenchallenge.org/centers/inland-empire/.

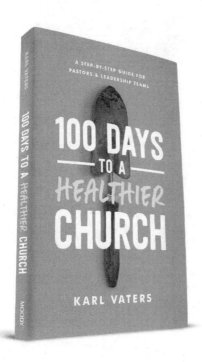

DO YOU LEAD A SMALL CHURCH?

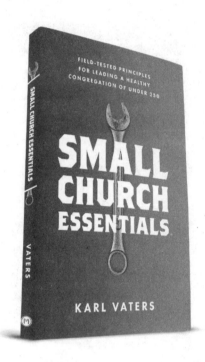

GET THE RESOURCES YOU NEED FOR WHEN LIFE TAKES AN UNEXPECTED TURN.

5 SIMPLE WAYS TO STRENGTHEN YOUR MARRIAGE
...When You're Stuck at Home Together
Gary Chapman

978-0-8024-2332-0

PSALMS FOR THE ANXIOUS HEART
A 30-Day Devotional for Uncertain Times
Becky Harling

978-0-8024-2338-2

WHAT NOW?
How to Move into Your Next Season
Mark Jobe

978-0-8024-2341-2

THE CHURCH RECOVERY GUIDE
How Your Congregation Can Adapt and Thrive after a Crisis
Karl Vaters

978-0-8024-2343-6

open THE BIBLE *in 30 days*
Colin S. Smith

978-0-8024-2344-3

PANDEMICS, PLAGUES, AND NATURAL DISASTERS
What is GOD Saying to Us?
Erwin W. Lutzer

978-0-8024-2345-0

HOW TO PRAY IN A CRISIS
A 4-Step Guide to Renewal
Daniel Henderson

978-0-8024-2359-7

WITHOUT A DOUBT
How to Know for Certain That You're Good with God
Dean Inserra

978-0-8024-2360-3

Be it in the midst of a natural disaster, global unrest, or an unforeseen pandemic, the repercussions of unprecedented change can leave us all reeling. Get the wisdom, encouragement, and peace you need to ease your anxieties, strengthen your relationships, and encounter the almighty God during such trying times.

also available as eBooks

MOODY Publishers®

From the Word to Life®